CUMMISKEY ALLEY

ALLEY

NEW AND SELECTED LOWELL POEMS

CUMMISKEY ALLEY

ALLEY

NEW AND SELECTED LOWELL POEMS

TOM
SEXTON

Loom Press
Lowell & Amesbury
Massachusetts
2020

Cummiskey Alley: New And Selected Lowell Poems
Copyright © 2020 by Tom Sexton

ISBN   978-1-7351689-1-3

Published in the United States of America
First Edition

Several of the poems in section one appeared on a popular blog in Lowell, Massachusetts, www.RichardHowe.com, as well as in *Cirque* and the anthology *Atlantic Currents: Connecting Cork and Lowell* (Loom Press, 2020). Most of the other poems appeared in the collections *A Clock with No Hands* (Adastra Press, 2007) and *Bridge Street at Dusk* (Loom Press, 2012). Many have been revised.

Loom Press, P.O. Box 1394, Lowell, MA 01853 and
15 Atlantic View, Amesbury, MA 01913
www.loompress.com
info@loompress.com

Design: Dennis Ludvino

Printing: King Printing Co., Inc., Lowell, Massachusetts

Cover photograph: "Commuters, Lowell, Mass., 1941" by Jack Delano, Library of Congress Collection

Author photograph: Kevin Harkins

Typefaces: Garamond Premier Pro and Filosofia

For those who have and for those who will call Lowell their home.

ALSO BY TOM SEXTON

Terra Incognita

Late August on the Kenai River

The Bend Toward Asia

A Blossom of Snow

Leaving for a Year

Autumn in the Alaska Range

World Brimming Over

The Lowell Poems

A Clock with No Hands

Crows on Bare Branches

For the Sake of the Light: New and Selected Poems

I Think Again of Those Ancient Chinese Poets

A Ladder of Cranes

Li Bai Rides a Celestial Dolphin Home

Snowy Egret Rising

CONTENTS

2 .

from
A CLOCK WITH NO HANDS

3.

from

BRIDGE STREET AT DUSK

4.

ON BECOMING A POET

I happened to be at the first factory just as the dinner hour was over, and the girls were returning to their work; indeed the stairs of the mill were thronged with them as I ascended. They were all well dressed, but not to my thinking above their condition; for I like to see the humbler classes of society careful of their dress and appearance.

— from *American Notes* by Charles Dickens (1844)

1.

NEW POEMS

Monotype of the Concord River Mills

Far from the print hanging on my wall,
a few battered old brick mills remain.
A tree grows from the sagging roof
of one as if its roots can keep a wall
from falling into the river below,
but in the print every brick glows
as if a mason has shaped it from light.
Is that bridge made of cloud or granite?
Inside one of the buildings, my mother
is about to meet my father for the first time.
Look how her auburn hair falls over one eye.
All the looms are singing. This I know to be true.

Mill Girls, Lowell, Mass., 1830

At dusk they could be seen through tall
windows, moth-like figures moving from loom
to loom in light cast by whale-oil lamps,
or when whale-oil was difficult to obtain
by the light of oil pressed from olives,
or when desperate, light from rendered fat
so they could spin then weave the rough-
cloth the mill owners shipped south
for plantation slaves to wear, a virtuous circle
if you held the lash or filled the ledger book.
They stayed three or four years just long
enough for a brother to finish college, or to add
a few acres to their family's worn out farm,
or save enough so they could open a shop.
Stay longer and their lungs were smudged lamps
half-filled with oily cotton dust, and in their ears
the ceaseless pounding of the looms that "sounded like
crickets" no matter how far from Lowell they travelled.

* The Lowell mill girls first went on strike for better working
  conditions in 1834.

Costello's Field

"The life of the universe in cosmic time
is briefer than that of a firefly," the scientist
on the stage is saying in answer to a question.
"Cosmic not sidereal time is my measure."
Suddenly I'm eight and running along the edge
of Costello's field after supper trying to catch
fireflies in a jar with holes punched in its cover.
The grass is damp. The stars overhead uncountable.

Cassandra

Lincolnville Beach, Maine

When the day's last ferry from Islesboro
docked and our car rolled down the ramp,
a woman, a fellow seafarer,
walked over and tapped on our window.
She must have noticed our license plate
with it standing brown bear.
"Stay on the coast, all the rest of Maine
is mill town where half of the people
are toothless as an egg," she whispered,
and then she walked back to her Mercedes.

I thought again of the half-deserted streets
of my Massachusetts hometown,
of the swing of a wrecking ball,
of bricks carried away for suburban patios,
of a neighbor toothless as an egg,
of the colors the tannery dyed the river.
If I'd spoken, she would've known I drop my r's
and had me dead to rights: mill town,
so I swallowed my tongue, nodded.
It was a beautiful day. What else could I do?

Good Friday

When I was a boy, I believed that if I was hit
by a car or fell into a canal, unlikely because
only adults did that and only late at night,
while I was walking to St. Patrick's church
in silence to make the Stations of the Cross
during the hours when poor Jesus was dying,
and if it was clear that I had but minutes
to live, a priest could be summoned from
Holy Trinity, the gold-domed Greek
Orthodox church not far from St. Patrick's
to give me the Last Rites of the *one true church*.

While I walked along, I imagined myself
lying bloodied in the gutter surrounded
by twelve weeping strangers who thought
the faint trace of a smile on my face
was a dying boy's first glimpse of heaven.
Lying there, I knew it was already too late
for even a sprinter to run over to St. Patrick's,
and I'd soon be walking down a street paved
with gold leading to a place where Greeks
live in mansions and dine on roast lamb,
rosemary potatoes and that fabulous egg-lemon
soup I had tasted once, all that followed
by belly dancers, while over in Heaven's Irish
neighborhood they would be eating mutton,
potatoes boiled to mush and soggy canned peas
followed by someone's little sister step dancing,
but nothing happened. I reached St. Patrick's
where two old biddies in black watched me move
from Station to Station, tears welling up in my eyes.

My Father Smoking a Camel

He's at our kitchen's small Formica table
smoking another cigarette at 1 a.m.
A caterpillar of pale ash on his saucer.
He's just gotten home from the corner bar
where he stops after work for an hour or two.
He seems to be studying the camel
and then the distant pyramids on the pack.
Six years ago we buried his wife, my mother.

I'd come down from sitting on my Goodwill cot
trying to understand a poem by Robert Lowell
about his father and enjoying the irony
of being born in a city named for his family.
My community college instructor assigned it.
What is the *Napoleon Book? Where is Mattapoisett?*

Aunt Irene's Peach Tree

It was in the side yard of the bungalow
where my Aunt Irene lived by the Merrimack River.
There she raised her brothers and sisters,
their parents dead long before their time to go.
I remember its fruit was small, but to a child
it was a treasure. I planted a pit wherever
we were living fall after fall, but a seedling never
sprouted in soil that was either too wet or too hard.

Aunt Irene and my mother would sit on the porch
and talk. Irene's head tilting like a priest's
hearing confession, one hand on my mother's knee.
I watched insects batter the torn screen door
while I rubbed the pit hidden in my pocket,
a pit I was convinced contained a magical seed.

Triangle Luncheonette

With its gleaming black-and-white marble floor
and even its exotic name, Luncheonette,
it could never be mistaken for a lowly diner
like the Club Diner on Dutton Street.
On my fifteen-minute break from work,
I sat at the Triangle's counter and ordered
a fried baloney sandwich on a Bulkie roll.

Your order was ready when the baloney
began to pop on the grill and its edges slowly
darkened and began to curl, then the cook
lifted it from the grill, added a little mustard
and slid it down the counter with a flourish.
I imagined sharing one with my not-yet girlfriend,
who, a bit of mustard on her teeth, would fall in love.

The Last Sunday Train, 1952

Little did I know trying to keep up with my father
as we walked toward Boston's old North Station
after watching Warren Spahn and Johnny Sain
pitch a doubleheader, that our team, the Boston
Braves, would soon be calling Milwaukee home.
We had free tickets given to us by a neighbor.
Six people were on the bullet-shaped train
when it finally pulled out of the station:
a man who had missed the train to Montreal
and was grumbling about spending a night in Lowell,
a woman who I was certain was someone's maid,
her black dress and sturdy black shoes a giveaway,
 a sleepy conductor with one eye on a man
with a bottle of *Four Roses* not quite hidden
from sight in the side pocket of his rumpled suit,
me waving my Braves banner by the window
and my father who was anxious to get home
because he had to be at work early in the morning.
Four Roses squinted at me and said with a smile
"A long time ago the Braves were the Beaneaters."
He said this as if he was telling me a great secret.
That caught the attention of Montreal who
seemed to think Beaneaters might be an insult
aimed at him like peasouper, pepsi, and frog.
He glared at Four Roses and the maid moved
to the back to be closer to the conductor.
My father suggested Four Roses pass the bottle
around and everyone seemed to like the idea.
He glanced at me and after taking a sip passed
the whiskey to the now wide-awake conductor.

Before long, led by a now smiling Montreal,
they were swaying with the car past dark station
after dark station, past dark field after dark field,
singing "Spahn and Sain and pray for rain."
It was a lament, or so it seems to me now,
as we rode our earthbound comet toward Lowell
and its Victorian depot that would soon be torn down.

Leaving Lowell for San Francisco, 1915, a Postcard

Standing beside Mayor Murphy on the steps
of City Hall, they seem far too young to shave:
The Cohens, Ellie and Max, and their friend
Max Greenberg. They will soon leave Lowell's
towering smokestacks far behind to begin
their long trek west to the Golden Gate.
Did they sleep beside the peddler's cart
that holds the postcards they planned to sell
to finance their dream of owning a store?

This postcard is all that we know of their quest.
Did they break bread with the wrong people
or fall out and go their separate ways
too embarrassed to send even a postcard home?
Did a fierce storm trap them in the Rockies?
Let us hope they reached San Francisco at dawn
with the sun on their shoulders like a shawl.

Coal

It's the early 1930's and Mr. Farley's driving
his black Packard 12, the finest car that will
ever be made, over Pleasant Street's cobbles.
They're on a cloud the way the Packard rides.
Mr. Farley has become a rich man selling coal,
the finest anthracite shipped from Pennsylvania.
He waves to the men walking to the tannery.
It's wise to smile and wave at your customers.
He feels good that he recognized the small man
who bought coal oil to cure his infant daughter.
The lunch pails they carry are as black as coal.
I could have been an artist Mr. Farley muses.
A man who looks like a human raccoon waves
from one of Mr. Farley's trucks. He smiles.
"The world will always need coal, Mrs. Farley,"
he tells Mrs. Farley sitting in the back, all in black.

Milkman

The sound of a truck's door sliding
open before the sun hit cobblestone
followed by footsteps on the back stairs
light as a cat's or even a ghost's, then
the bell-like sound of empty milk bottles
being picked up and quickly replaced
by a shadowy man who never fails to deliver,
a joke milkmen share with each other
at 4 a.m. while loading their Delco trucks.
Milkmen who appeared even when snow thicker
than cream on the top of a bottle was falling.
His lights glowing like the eyes of a snowy owl.

Race Walker

He was always almost running, almost walking
like a puppet attached to invisible strings
as he climbed the steep hill from the tannery
that before long would close its doors for good.
I say puppet because one foot was always
planted on the ground while the other foot
seemed to dangle in the air before he set it down.

He was a comic figure to the men who walked
to work then walked back home at dusk,
dreaming of buying a used car before too long,
perhaps a Ford coupe or a green Hudson Hornet.
He looked neither to his left nor to his right
but kept his eyes on something just out of sight.

Angela Poses for Her Photograph

Grapes ripen on the vines behind Angela
who has placed her left arm around the waist
of a terra cotta cherub. It's her birthday
present from her husband, Joe, who "brought
her over from Italy in '51 to work beside him."
Two days later she was beside him in the mill.
"She's never missed a single day, not even one."

She's survived more than her share of trouble.
Two children dead before they had a sip of wine.
Cancer knocking on the door. Shots in the alley.
The evening light catches her hooped earrings
and the thin gold chain around one ankle.
The cherub seems delighted to be in the scene
to play even a small part in Angela's affirmation.

Sailor Tom's

Once a summer if money wasn't too tight
we took the winding road from Lowell
to Sailor Tom's. My father's driving was too slow
for me, I could get there faster on my bike.
Once there his steps on the gangplank were light.
I knew that after we finished eating, he'd go
have a drink with the owner and his pet crow.
They had worked together and were still tight.

Everything was possible on that restaurant ship.
Its immigrant owner's dream had come true.
Why not ours? My mother gave her hair a flip
as if to say we'll give our troubles the slip
this time for sure. No more singing the blues.
Chief Pontiac on our prow would bring us safely home.

Mr. Nolan's Hedge

Wearing the bright green Tyrolian hat
his German war bride made for him,
Mr. Nolan trimmed his privacy hedge
Wednesday after Wednesday
when the bank where he was head-teller
locked its heavy doors at noon.
At exactly 12:10 p.m. we heard, clip, clip.
A carpenter could have used it as a level.

He had a dream job, an obedient wife,
so it came as a surprise when one Sunday
morning he was found asleep on his hedge
without his hat by a neighbor on her way
to early Mass. "What else would you expect
with a German wife," they whispered up and
down the block. She heard. They moved away.
Before long cats where hunting in the hedge.

The Man in the Moon

When I was a boy, I thought the Man
in the Moon was looking down
with a smile on his face; when I asked
my father why, he said, "because
he's had a little claret for his supper,
it keeps him warm and smiling."
It must be cold up there without a scarf,
I thought, then looking up I smiled.

Looking back now, when steam was rising
from the power plant down the block,
it did make the Man in the Moon
seem to be a little wobbly, like my father
coming up Oak Street hill late for supper
wearing his *I've had a few beers* grin
while my mother ladled out cold stew
before, unsmiling, she sent me off to bed.

O'Toole

Some memories, welcome or not, never fade:
O'Toole appeared one October, his face as worn
as an old man's. He was as cautious as a stray
at recess. Were his too short trousers always torn?
His seat in class was empty by December.
The house where he lived, the sagging
one on Fayette Street by the Concord River
was empty. Did he ever dream of better days?

This image of him sticks to me like a burr:
He's sitting on the icy stairs to that house.
It's snowing. He doesn't have a sweater
never mind a coat. All the lights are out.
Did he call my name as I rushed by
pretending to look at something in the sky?

White Sheep of the Family

Once, in a town not too far away
from here, there was a family
that seemed to always be in trouble:
a few pills sold, a missing car found
behind their house covered with a tarp,
a little protection offered for a lottery ticket.

Even their sainted mother was known
to leave the neighborhood store with a few
things she'd somehow forgotten to pay for.
The sons might break a stranger's jaw.
The daughters might kneel you in the groin.
Turn around if you see them on the sidewalk.

The youngest son became a civil servant
and was in all things gracious, civil.
He'd open doors for women and for men,
sweep his elderly neighbor's walk.
Answer any foolish question with a smile.
No one it seems ever saw him frown.

After a few beers at the kitchen table
when he'd excused himself for a moment,
the others would look at each other and begin
to sing with a slowly rising chorus:
"baa baa white sheep have you any,"
then after a very long pause, they'd add, "balls."

It was said he resembled his absent father,
the only one who did, the father who went to work

one Sunday morning and never returned.
From time to time someone would say
they saw him in South Boston or Reno.
He'll come back when he's ready, they said.

Home Room

8 a.m. My second year in a freshman
homeroom, the only one beginning to shave,
out of place in my yellow pegged pants, hand-
me-downs Ray True was about to throw away.
I was cool only to the Greek girl who sat
behind me trying out her still exotic English:
tonic, bus token, frappe, cold water flat,
all new words treasured like a granted wish.

I was tongue-tied almost unable to speak
to her or to anyone who wore a dress.
When she whispered to me, my knees went weak.
Was my treasured Greaser's haircut a mess?
Where is she now my olive-skinned muse
who stole my heart without leaving a bruise?

Sirens

In the summer of the year the Korean Conflict
began a non-war that took older brothers away,
we crossed a bridge over the Concord River
to a shallow canal more than a mile from
the Immaculate Conception, our parish.
Girls from St. Peter's Parish wearing only
their panties and bras swam in that canal.
To us they were the Sirens on their rock
singing to sailors lashed to a broken mast
like the ones painted on the white-washed
walls of the Greek restaurant on Market Street.
All summer long, we were those brave Greeks
lashed to desire sailing over treacherous water
not quite knowing what to do if we heard their song
or if one of them should show a snow-white breast.

Catcher

In memory of Jay McHale, 1940–2017

I can still see your thin frame behind the plate
when Little League baseball came to Lowell.
I don't remember the teams, but the year
was 1952. I do remember tripping in a hole
during tryouts when my name was called.
I was weak at bat and not much in the field.
You were flawless behind the plate calling
a game, certain no one would ever steal
a base on you or hit one over the fence.
I know we're old men and you're not well,
but luminous memories are our best defense
against what's coming, heaven, nothing, hell.
You've just thrown a runner out at third base
with one flawless motion, with effortless grace.

Work

It was always scarce, a few piece-work jobs
in a shoe shop or at least that was the rumor.
1958 was anything but a very good year.
Fresh out of school, we lingered on the corner
of Merrimack and Central looking for work,
but it never came by. That was our joke.
We knew we were headed for the military.
If we were lucky, Big Al, who was a body man
and never out of work even though he never
finished the eighth grade, some said seventh,
appeared in his chopped and channeled Ford
and offered to drive one or maybe two of us
around the block with the windows down,
moving at a snail's pace so we could be seen.

In Praise of the Graveyard Shift

Whoever named it never walked out of an old brick
building at 6 a.m. to bird song and a sky not blue
but white like a China plate used only on holidays,
or watched the stars overhead during a break,
or saw how mist on an old car's paint can make
it seem almost new, or felt cold chrome on their palm
when opening the driver's door after a good night's work
that paid the bills and left a little over for the ponies.

Whoever named it never stopped at the small diner
down the road, the bullet-shaped one on a riverbank,
where after your face was known, a waitress would
set your mug of coffee with cream and sugar down
on the counter before you then scribble your silent
order on a blue-lined pad, a kind of benediction.

Concord River Carp
for Mike Casey

The last
section of

trail that
will be

when it's
done an

art walk
with lines

of poetry
etched in

granite a
little prose

will be
there too

but now
it ends

at an
old factory

now used
as housing

for the
elderly, where

two women,
sat on

a bench
by the

river having
a smoke

at 5:00
a.m.

One looked
at me

when I
asked her

about a
bridge that

was there
years ago

she said
while her

friend gazed

at the

budding trees.
"For three

years two
carp came

to me
every morning,

they were
so beautiful

magical, one
nibbled Wonder

Bread From
my fingers,

no carp
this year,

the wrong
kind of

people are
coming down

our trail
now, drunks

were better,
not the

druggies never.
They say

they're artists
but they

want this
spot here

for a
statue or

for them"
then deciding

I probably
didn't have

a hook
for a

tongue said
"I think

they might
be lovers."

In Honor of Those Who Served, 1898–1902

It's Saturday afternoon, downtown's empty
except for those walking to apartments
in buildings where new immigrants live.
I'm watching a man and a boy, laughing,
calling out to each other in Spanish,
chasing each other around the now green
statue of a soldier on the auditorium's grass.
Out of breath, they stop to examine the plaque
in the shape of a cross that honors the boys
from Lowell who defeated the Spanish in Cuba,
then the Philippine rebels, finally the Chinese Boxers:
"Not A War For Conquest Or For Military Glory
But A Righteous War To Succor The Weak And
Oppressed" it proclaims to all who stop to read.
He takes the boy's hand, they laugh, begin to run.

Cummiskey Alley

It's Sunday morning with church bells ringing
as a family speaking Spanish rushes by me
in this narrow alley named for Hugh Cummiskey
the Irishman who led his crew of "white niggers"
thirty miles from Charlestown to dig the canals
that made Lowell's mills the envy of the world.
Old buildings on both sides of the alley sag.

When I reach the Market Street end, a man
sitting in a Caddy with all its windows down
is listening to a talk show host with a Boston-Irish
accent loudly praising President Trump's wall.
"Send them all back, send them all to hell,"
he shouts, then, smiling, looks at me and says,
"The bastards never even try to learn the language."

A few blocks away from where he's parked his Caddy
a Yankee mob tried in 1831 to burn St. Patrick's
church to the ground and drive the Irish out of town,
a mob driven back to town in a panic
by Irish women who had armed themselves with
paving stones, stones they carried in their aprons.

Letting Them Go

"Once when a swan landed on the river in a snow
storm I thought it was the Holy Ghost,"
my mother says as I loosen the rope around
her neck so my uncle can't find and cut her down.
I tell her Grandmother Farrell's going to read
the leaves in your cup in an hour so we need to leave
this damp cellar and get to her house. She smiles
and says, "We better get going it's a good walk."

And what am I to do with my poor father alone
in that coffin-sized room? Silent as a stone
when he was alive, alone on the night he died.
Turning from the window, he looks at me and sighs,
"Please don't put me in any more of your sad poems.
You've always been melancholy to the bone."
He seems content to be dead. I feel relieved.
When I get up to go, he asks, "Anything you need?"

The Heart in Winter

All it wants is for me to raise the window shade
when I get up so we can see what's going on
then have a cup or two of coffee to get us going
while we wait for memory's gate to swing open.
Today I'm the first to appear wearing blue suede
shoes and a pink shirt with a white collar.
I can't dance, but I do a little step for the mirror.
There's a bucketful of Brylcreem in my hair.
Is this the night you'll be broken for the first time?
I ask. "Look how young we were," he sighs.

Cawley Stadium, 1956

At halftime when the teams had left the field
Thelma, if that was her name, would appear
with a girlfriend on either side to begin a slow
walk around the football field's four sides.
She would have made Jayne Mansfield gasp
if Mansfield had been watching from the stands.
Was she a high school student or was she older?
The trees beyond the stadium were blushing.

Wearing a white apron and carrying a box of ice
cream bars, I followed them from section to section.
"Thelma, Thelma" rising from the stands as Thelma
throwing her shoulders back or offering a faint smile
passed by, then I'd hear an embarrassed "ice cream
over here" from men who later had to ask the score.

My 50's Porkpie Fedora

Less than a month out of Uncle Sam's army
and still sporting a crew cut, I was handed a slip
of paper by a clerk at the unemployment office
where I had gone to draw my very first check
and told to get it signed at the personnel office
at the mill where he told me to go for an interview.
I was to return it the following week if not hired.
I said something about being a personnel specialist
not a laborer. He called the name of the next in line.

I wore my overcoat and my 50's porkpie fedora
to the interview, and I carried my sister's umbrella.
The man who did the hiring walked me through
a long room where women sat before machines.
I'm sure we took that walk for their amusement.
A few smiled so I bowed then tipped my fedora.
Back in his office, he gave me a conspiratorial grin
then wrote, "Right now we got no work for him."

2 a.m.

I was looking down from my room on the second floor
of a small town's only hotel because I couldn't sleep.
A man wearing Coke-bottle glasses that made him
look like an owl was trying to keep his balance
as he walked the empty street's fading center line
like Nik Wallenda crossing Niagara Falls on a wire.
He glanced up and seeing me at my open window
called out, "I'm the only one holding it all together,"
before he swayed, caught his balance, moved on.

Always Worse Down River

Even when crack cocaine was gutting block
after block, people in Lowell would say with
pride it's much worse down river in Lawrence
where empty mills shadow every street
and the Merrimack's full of cars driven out
on the ice and stripped of everything
worth a nickel before they go to the bottom.
The river's blacker than a drug dealer's heart
down there so they'll never find the cars
or the skeleton sitting in the passenger's seat
with a single bullet hole in the back of its skull.
Granted no one's found a body yet but they will.
In Lowell you might find a washing machine
or a tire with pretty good tread on a usable rim.

Willie Provencher's Ghost

"I'm not sure what the hell I'm doing here,"
Willie says, looking around the pool room.
"I'm dead and the air's too goddamned clear,
no cigarette smoke, and it's clean as a tomb.
Everywhere I look tattooed women and men
playing together, two guys holding hands."
One of the women asks Willie if he wants in.
"Eight ball," she says. It's almost a demand.

Her fat wallet soon empty, she slinks away.
Everyone else is looking out the window.
Willie sighs, "Minnows," then looks my way.
"Alaska my ass," he says, "get me home.
I miss Maloof and his shiny black shoes
that squeak every time I'm about to shoot."

A Sad Tune

We rode a series of busses from home
to Nashua so my mother could visit
a chiropractor, they were not welcome
in 1940's Massachusetts, but my
mother was desperate to ease the pain
from rheumatoid arthritis that turned
her easy smile to a painful grimace.
Grandmother Farrell had seen a rainbow
and a pot of gold when she read the leaves
on the bottom of my mother's empty cup.

That pot of gold was all my mother needed
to follow the advice of someone who knew
someone who might have been cured by
having gold injections from a chiropractor,
so off we went Friday after Friday.
She held my hand to ease her constant pain,
and for a time Grandmother Farrell's reading
seemed to be coming true, but in the end
nothing eased her pain for more than a day or two.
On our last long ride home, the bus's accordion doors
played a sad tune every time they opened or closed.

Remembering Lowell High School

On my first day, feeling a slight shiver,
I hurried down East Merrimack Street
then across the bridge over the Concord River
close to where Lowell's two rivers meet,
then toward the tall neon sign spelling out SUN
the modest name of our afternoon paper,
trying to remember my homeroom's number. 121?
I was a grammar schoolboy, parochial in every way.

Sometimes in my dreams, I'm walking a long hall
listening to young voices long forgotten,
or seeing a familiar face, a smile. Some will fall
far too young, full of promise or not;
but, for a time, unaware, we merged, became one.
I'll name only these: Wojas, Frazier, Cote, Anderson.*

* In 2018, I was asked to write a poem for the 60th reunion of my
  high school class.

Oak Street Revisited

Nostalgia's golden glow brings back the oaks
that lined the street, the door my parents stooped
to enter, brings back that deep November snow
falling as thick as sugar from a grocer's scoop.
School was canceled so I hurried up Oak Street hill
to the bus stop where I'd often look for change.
New snow was perfect for finding coins that spilled.
That morning it was quarters from a driver's changer.

I still remember digging them out, one by one,
an endless shaft of silver that numbed my fingers,
a treasure shown to my parents, not yet undone
by pain, by debt, by death's indifferent sting.
A pot of milk was soon heating on the stove
for hot chocolate with drifts of cream like snow.

2.

from

A CLOCK WITH NO HANDS

Oak Street in the Snow

I watch my father sliding down the hill
to our new house. He has let himself slide
like a child who is convinced he cannot fall
but will lift off from the ground and fly
in a wide circle over the house like a witch.
He went out to buy the proper tools to open
a hollow-sounding wall in our kitchen.
He has a hunch it hides a beehive oven.
By dark he has found his El Dorado:
the oven and a bean pot holding a coin.
He tells me how he slid downhill in the snow.
I buzz in his lap. He is not annoyed.
He will not die in a flop house "round noon."
Not while I hold him fast in that room.

Rogers Hall, 1947
for Anne Sexton

One night we climbed its tall fence
and ran across the endless lawn
of Rogers Hall that we had been told
was a boarding school for rich girls
who did "it" in the back seat of taxi cabs.

We ran from tree to tree toward
the building with the swimming pool
where older boys from the neighborhood
claimed to have seen girls swimming naked.
The watchman caught us soon enough.

Was that you, white-capped and sleek,
slicing through the blue-green water,
the one who saw us at the window,
or were you in your room writing poems
your mother claimed you plagiarized?

Our brothers swam in the canals
you had to cross to get downtown.
One year, a girl caught her foot
in a mattress spring on the bottom
of the canal where she was diving.

People watched her struggle from the bridge,
hands waving from just below the surface
until she turned her face away as if
embarrassed. Her body seemed as white
as chalk when they laid her on the bank.

She was a pieceworker who slipped
away from work to swim that afternoon.
Did you know? Would it have mattered?
Despair like water seeks its own level.
You dove too deep and it was waiting.

My Bedroom Window

When I woke, the arrow in the stove's gauge
was one of Robin Hood's fallen from his quiver.
No kerosene. My father had forgotten to pay.
My icy window would be my book that winter.
I would test myself and emerge a man of steel.
I watched Nanook armed with only a harpoon
inching across black ice toward a seal.
I traveled with Peary beneath an Arctic moon.

I was among the bravest of brave Shackleton's
crew locked in a world of endless ice.
The bones in my hands froze to the quick.
If I was going to die, I'd die with a smile.
Still, I was sad when I woke to a clear window
and a sapling unbending like an archer's bow.

Ragman

I wake to the singing of birds outside
my bedroom window. The air is sweet
with the scent of rain and blossoms
opening. And then I hear the odd clack
of wheels on cobbles, and I think again
of the grainy news reel and somber voice
saying, "Most of Europe's Jews perished."

"They killed Christ and have the devil's
tail beneath their coats," Mulligan said.
He heard Mr. Casey tell that to his father.
I watch the ragman, scarecrow thin
below me on the street. No horns. No tail.
He gets down and takes an apple from
his pocket for his horse, then they move on.
The wet cobbles like skulls in their wake.

The Lesson

If you hear someone coming up the stair
place the back of a chair under the doorknob
because the lock will not hold if pushed
with any force, do not answer even
a friendly voice for it could be that man
come back to take our new couch,
he must have misplaced our payment,
or it could be that sheriff with another
piece of paper to pester your father,
stay well away from the windows even
the one with the curtain for an hour
and if you see them on the street
cross over to the other side, be invisible
like that white rabbit in the magician's hat
and the Holy Ghost who watches over us.

The Red Sox Tree

It seemed to take all morning to go around
the massive trunk of that ancient beech.
Almost ten, I kept one eye on the ground
as I climbed as high as I could reach.
A vet who fought on Iwo Jima carved
their line-up where the branches thinned
far above the last initials in their heart
where the air was always cold on the skin.
Climbing to it was my goal that summer,
and on the Fourth I was almost there
when I was forced back down by thunder
and lightning close enough to singe my hair.
Safe at home behind my bedroom door,
I chanted Williams, Pesky and Bobby Doerr.

East Merrimack Street

I'm far too young to have heard of acrophobia
as I approach a bridge I'm afraid to cross.
I'm sure I'll fall into the river and be lost,
swept away for good by the rapids below.

When I reach the bridge, I say the names
carved on the building I just walked past.
Magical words I tell myself, from first to last.
Tripoli, Trenton, Shiloh. Lundy's Lane.

I shut my eyes tight and grip the rail.
Trenton. My hands are wet and cold.
Shiloh. No turtle ever moved so slow.
They won't find enough of me to fill a pail.

My hand grips air, so I open my eyes.
Tripoli, Lundy's Lane. I'm on the other side.

Paddy O'Conner

"We go because he's cheap," my father said,
but I'd heard he was a gunman for the IRA.
The English had put a price on his head
so big it would tempt even a brother.
They sent him to Lowell to be a barber
which explained why one of your ears
always seemed much lower than the other
when he spun you around to the mirror.

A dark man in a cloth cap was always there
watching Paddy sharpen his straight razor.
They pretended to talk about what they would do
if they won the Irish Sweepstakes. I knew better.
One word to me and I'd stand all day near
the window waiting for the hated English to appear.

Mr. Nason's Train

On Christmas Eve of the year Mr. Nason
came back from the Aleutian Islands
where he had fought the Japs who died
like rats deep in their booby-trapped caves,
he set up track in every room and gable
of his house. His wife watched with a sigh.
Was he a boy again watching the night sky
tilt as his train pulled out of the station?

Twice sent to my room, I couldn't sleep
a wink, so I got out of bed in the dark
to watch for Santa's sleigh from my window.
What I saw was Mr. Nason's train climbing a steep
grade toward a constellation of stars
he had pasted on the ceiling. I watched him go.

Grandmother Farrell

Memory is as
fragile and thin
as the shell
of a China cup
held to the light
by a curious child,
but I can see you
clearly tonight
at your kitchen table
between Madeline,
your daughter, who
saved for years
to buy a small
garage on a blind
curve with her
husband, Dusty True,
and my mother who
has yet to begin
her dark descent.

You're reading
the leaves on
the bottom of
my mother's cup
of tea, and
we're sitting
on your couch,
my long-legged
sister, who doesn't
know our

cousins call her
Raggedy Ann,
and me holding
your rosary
between two fingers.
I'm trying
to count the beads,
but I cannot
get beyond seven,
so I watch
you as you find
a pattern in the leaves.
In a whisper,
your voice too low
for me to hear.
Walking home with
the sound of the river
in our ears, our
beautiful auburn-
haired mother
weaves a tale
of a small house
with a peach
tree in the yard
and a car by the curb—
Overhead, the innocent
moon you summoned
from the dark.

Uncle Paul

I can still remember walking with him
and my father in the warehouse
where my Uncle Paul worked until
it shut down. We made the rounds
checking doors, punching clocks.

Work was scarce by the time I was ten.
Uncle Paul would sit in our almost empty front
room talking about moving to Arizona.
By the end of that September, he was dead.
He fell and broke his neck while picking apples.

The other pickers weren't the least surprised.
They thought he was strange at best. A small
man who picked only flawless apples leaving
tree after tree needing to be picked again.
The boss was going to can him on that Friday.

Sometimes when the cooling autumn air
pricks my skin like a baling hook,
I think of my Uncle Paul. It's Sunday.
He's sitting in the ancient Hupmobile
he bought somewhere for fifteen dollars.

My father's beside him in the front seat.
They're looking at a map with Paul's route
west marked out with thick red lines
as thick as the veins on the back of Paul's
hands, brothers dreaming of a new beginning.

1988-2019

Father

When the clerk after last week's rent
forced the locked door, it was almost
too late for the undertaker's

gaudy art. He left little behind
that day his death became official:
his razor and two crumpled one-

dollar bills. Crossing the Textile
Avenue Bridge after his hasty
wake, I watched a sad moon drag

its empty net across the river
and remembered the night a bartender
told me my father wanted to be a tenor

when they were boys. I never heard him sing.
Once below the dam, where I fished
for carp to sell to Polish women,

I hooked then lost a speckled fish
my friend Leo Paradis called a trout
before it slipped the hook

and fell back to the sluggish water.
A bright fish that made me want to sing.
Father, soon I will believe that fish was you.

1980-2019

The Great Flood of 1936

It happened four years before I was born
and even then it was talked about as if
it was a biblical event. A few sips from a fifth
and my uncle would say, "Water rushed down
from the mountains. The whole valley drowned,"
and it did. The best bloodhound couldn't sniff
out dry land. The high falls became a riffle.
The rushing river drowned out every other sound.

A table rushed by with supper still on it
followed by a child's coffin. My father always
told the story of the man who was holding
onto a roof when it hit a bridge and split.
Somehow he climbed to the top of the bridge
and looking down, like Noah, spit into the flood.

Mr. Moore's Car

It was painted the color of calf's liver
and might have been a hearse when new.
Every Sunday after Mass, Mr. Moore
adjusted the rear and sideview mirrors
and practiced backing into a space
on the empty street before his house
while Mrs. Moore watched from a window.

Satisfied the car was parallel to the curb,
he wiped it down as if it were the pony
he rode in Ireland when he was a lad,
then he locked it up and checked the trunk.
At night we would see his profile behind
lace curtains like a priest's behind a screen,
a priest who knows sinners roam the streets.

The Proper Balance

On those summer mornings when my father
was out on strike, we'd get up before dawn
and go street by street looking for scrap-metal
put out as trash, metal and other treasures.
Sometimes the road was full of deep puddles
as we drove block by block in our old Cadillac
that was always for sale. Water would come
through the holes in the floor. One morning
we found an ancient water heater that made
the junkman's scale moan as he added weight
upon weight trying to get the proper balance
complained all the time that he couldn't make
a penny paying such prices for lead and copper.

On the drive home from the junk yard
that morning, every light was green not red
and the Cadillac's radio stayed on even when
we hit a pothole that should have broken
its rusting frame. When Father James, our
landlord, climbed the stairs after saying Mass,
the rent was paid on time for once, and the wine
we kept for company stayed quiet in its bottle.

The Slap

That morning I put on my mother's dress
and high heels and smeared lipstick on my face
the way I'd seen beloved Uncle Milty do
on the Duffy's television before I hurried
down the stairs to try to make her smile.
One slap and an angry "Take it off now."
Nothing else. Wearing a dress must be
a serious sin I thought, one I didn't know.

With thunder in my head, I ran and ran
trying not to step on a single crack
afraid I'd break my mother's back
and I'd hurt her far too much already.
My mother never mentioned the dress again.
But I knew the ice we skated on was thin.

Mike Rynne

The bathhouse and a race are named for him
now, but I remember a man well past his prime
who towed a boat with seven hefty friends in it
across the Merrimack River. They made it rise.
Neighbors said he trained by eating raw oysters
washed down with whiskey if someone stood
the bill or drank to our boys fighting in Korea.
An Irishman welcome in every neighborhood.
His friends tightened his thick leather harness
before he began to swim. I stood on the far bank
with my father, and all we could see were arms
rising white from water that was murky and rank.
Suddenly he stood there like a god in the shallows,
and nothing at all could make the day ring hollow.

Aunt Irene

She rose before dawn in the small house
where she raised her brothers and sisters
and climbed the steep hill that led to Mrs.
Costello's kitchen day after day without
complaint. If she bent to hold us close,
lilac scented her blouse, and a fine mist
of lilac filled her house. Radiators hissed
welcome when we appeared out of the cold.
We waited for her to come down at night
with something for us from that ample kitchen:
a jar from S.S. Pierce with a lion on the label,
I hoped. Some nights I turned on all the lights
to help her find her way down through the mist
that rose from the river thick as that lion's mane.

Hornpout

Moving my father's flashlight back and forth
over the wet grass, I looked for nightcrawlers
that were too far out of their holes to go back
down when they sensed I was approaching.
Tomorrow I would catch my first hornpout
in a deep pool a little below Scripture's laundry,
a place where poisonous black snakes hid
in the rocks. It was best to go before it got warm.

While I waited nervously for my bobber to go
under, I thought of the horns around its mouth.
I'd been told they would cut me to the bone,
but what I remember now is the color of its belly
when it rolled and tried to go back to the bottom.
Moon-yellow like the cream on the top of a bottle.

The Night We Played McNamara's Band

Even Marilyn M who would never be
graceful didn't stumble when we took our
places on the stage, nor did Martha D
who was painfully shy and thin as a sliver.

On my left, was lanky Rita McG
who become the girlfriend of a murderer.
She held my hand to calm my shaking knees.
Leo P's cowlick stood up like a hurdle.

When Sister R signaled from her seat
we put lips to combs covered with waxed paper.
Her foot tapped one, two, three, one, two, three.
A whispered "play as one" promised ice cream later.

And who in that Parish Hall was not amazed
when a passable harmony rose from that stage?

Lucy Larcom Park

Leaving the boarding house run by her mother
she walked the wide avenue to the mill
pausing to smile at a girl listening to the trill
of a robin. They wrote verse for each other
at the end of the day counting out meter
on bobbin-weary fingers. Which syllables
should be stressed and which bent to their will?
Would her humble verse please Mr. Whittier?

Or so I imagined her as I walked through
the park, thinking of her so I would forget
that most of her world had been turned to dust.
"Lowell goes in a loom and Lynn in a shoe"
sage Emerson wrote. But witty trope or not
in the end what doesn't fall will rust.

Elevator Operator

Someone jacked off on a nurse's uniform
late one night, so I had to take a lie detector
test or be fired. One janitor went home.
I passed. Boss's nephew, the one with the fat neck,
confessed. Those cars took skill. I'm no clown.
Christmas after Christmas drunken partygoers
slurring "This job must have its ups and downs"
needed my arm in getting out the door.
They all forgot my name by New Year's Eve.
One morning I took a lawyer down a peg or two.
He said I was late to his floor and yanked my sleeve.
Next time I stopped below his floor and out he flew.
Automatic now. I remember polishing the door
and the echo of my taps on the marble floor.

Harry Bass

I still remember the Sunday morning
he chose me to be his caddy. Harry,
who wore a black patch over one eye
and swung a driver like a fly swatter,
was one of Longmeadow's token Jews
who always seemed to play together.
I cut a hole in my pocket so I could
let a new ball snake down my leg while
I walked to the fairway from the rough
where his drive almost always landed.
His partners knew what was going on
if Harry didn't. No matter how hot or cold
the day, they had come to expect we'd find
Harry's ball, as bright as a New World whose
promise hadn't faded, sitting in the fairway.

Mill Towns

When the owners chain the gates for good
and leave for Southeast Asia with a shrug,
the towns begin to fall like dominoes
one by one. Notice the old triple deckers
leaning together like grandmothers
who've seen the young follow a Pied-
Piper out of town and never return.
That man sitting alone in a worn booth
at the back of the Main Street Diner
is holding a letter from his son.
Babylon, he thinks, the Tigris River.
He'll finish the cold coffee in his cup
when the whistle blows his phantom shift.
Once back in his rented room by the mill,
he'll put the letter in the old bureau
where he keeps his medals from another war.

Grey Nuns of the Sacred Heart

They blend in memory now, the kind, the good,
those who belonged behind the convent walls
down on their knees scrubbing the floors
that, if chosen, we scrubbed on Saturday morning
hoping to catch a glimpse of a nun with her
head uncovered. Did they really shave their heads
and crawl on glass shards until their knees were raw
and as bloody as a heart pierced by a lance?

What of Sister Rose of Lima, named for a saint
who wore a spiked crown concealed by roses
and slept on a bed of thorns, Sister who led us
from school to church with her hands folded
in prayer while we mocked her behind her back
before one by one, by one, we slipped away.

White-Tail Deer

Deer were never seen in downtown Lowell,
but that afternoon one was spotted trying
to cross the Concord River on thin ice.
No rack, so it must have been a doe.
We stood bathed in a cruiser's eerie glow
watching it slip and fall then somehow rise
and move toward the open water on the side
closest to the shore where the current's flow
was strong, and then we heard the black ice
crack. It stood motionless as a marble statue
before with one leap it cleared the water in slow
motion then scrambled up the bank and out of sight
between two buildings where they once made gears,
and when the new moon rose, it was that doe.

Memoir

"To dispel my melancholy, I write another poem."
—Tu Fu

I read that line many years ago
and imagined melancholy as an old sweater
worn and thinning at the elbows,
a dark conceit to be used one day.
Today is the winter solstice.
The light had barely touched the ground
when I left the house to check the mail.

There I found my sister's unexpected memoir
and discovered that we have different fathers,
hers revealed by an aunt in her cups
and that our mother hanged herself in our damp cellar,
a place where she was afraid to go,
when I was far from home learning how to be a soldier.
I've pulled on that sweater to keep out the cold.

Dark Hands Webbing Time

In a park where I once played ball all day
I stop to watch a pickup baseball game.
The players are speaking an Asian tongue.
Vietnamese I wonder? Their hands as dark
as the gloves they wear. One offers me a glove
and points to right field with a knowing smile.
How did he know that was my position?
For a moment, I'm a boy loping across new
grass toward a Spaulding white as snow
before I shake my head no and move on
into a daydream where I catch it in the webbing
of my outstretched glove before I turn and throw
it home, a double play, man cut down at the plate.

Trolls

How long after they came back
from the war
the first one appeared under the bridge,
no one is certain.
People crossing would look down
and see them fishing
or smoking tobacco wrapped in brown paper.
They never seemed to leave.
There was talk.
Their wives and children quickly learned
to look away.
After all they seldom if ever came home.
No one seemed to know
when the first body appeared down river
in an eddy and then another
caught on the lip of an unused dam.
No matter how many were hooked and pulled
from the murky water, others took their place;
and like roiling high water in the spring,
they came to be expected.

Mary Shiels
Eastport, Maine

I've placed a cut branch of winterberry
on your grave and another beside the lamb
that marks your daughter's resting place.
Their berries glow like a lantern's welcome.
Who carved "A native of County Wexford,
Ireland" beneath your name for all to read?
Those words remain firm and clear after
more than a century of wind and icy storms.

From where I stand at the foot of your grave,
I can see Canada's Deer Island out in the bay.
A handful of songbirds sheathed in ice plunged
into the dory of one of her fishermen
when he was caught out in a storm last year.
He put them under his heavy sweater.
Only one survived the night in the makeshift
cage he placed beside his glowing stove.
The moon that saw your birth is now rising
out of the bay to touch your stone.
It's Samhain Eve and time for me to go.

On Milltown Boulevard

St. Stephen, New Brunswick

When I left the dentist's office
a Christmas parade was passing by.
I watched a beauty queen shivering
in the back seat of a convertible
new when shutdowns were unknown
and cars always clogged the road.
The thrift store had two tables outside
where sweaters muttered to each other.

The people around me began to cheer
when a truck carrying Boy Scouts appeared.
One of the scouts had the severed head
of a coyote attached to the end of a pole.
As if to acknowledge the rising cheers
the coyote nodded to the left and to the right.
On the truck behind the scouts, a wide-eyed
Santa Claus threw candy to the crowd.

The Flight

The sound of geese high above the house
when he woke from another restless sleep,
the sleep of the old, he told himself.
If he happened to wake during the night
when he was a child, the man across the alley
would be sitting at his kitchen table,
a man who worked in the mill with his father.
There was something ghostly about the scene:
a man in a white undershirt sitting in the
light cast by a bulb hanging from a wire;
no matter what time it was when he woke,
the man was there in that odd colorless light.
Slipping out of bed without waking his wife,
he went downstairs and then out into the yard
where he slowly raised and lowered his pale
arms until they were covered with down.

Snooker

Cigarette smoke filled the hall where he
sat with a rack in one massive hand.
He shaved his head and seldom spoke.
No one ever tried to stiff him for a game.
He was our South End Antaeus who drew
his strength from the hall and not the earth.
When a game was over, he racked the balls
with a rolling motion that sounded like thunder.

After a condemned sign was nailed to the door
and plywood nailed over every window,
a neighbor who had a key found him inside
curled up on one of his prized snooker tables
like a child who put his head down on the grass
to sleep. His brains were splattered over the floor.

Laundry Workers

They were the thin shouldered women
we saw crossing the Rogers Street Bridge
day after day when the sun was coming up
and we were out of school for the summer.
They stood in line outside the laundry's door
waiting for the whistle to call them inside
to a long day of endless heat and steam
and a boss who might fire them for nothing.
From our hiding place across the river
were we smoked and gambled for bottle caps,
we watched them raise their weary arms
to square and fold newly laundered sheets
white as our sisters' First Communion dresses.
From time to time one would hold a fresh shirt
close while she danced slowly for the others
with a grace far beyond our comprehending.
Watching her move from window to window
with the shirt clinging like a ghostly lover,
we were far too young to know desire,
but we sensed the sorrow in that dancing.
A continent and more than a half a century away,
I watch them crossing that bridge in single file.

Ducharme

Ducharme always moved across the ring
like a massive ox yoked to a heavy plow.
He won by knockout or heard "the birdies sing"
he said. He dreamt of being another Marciano.
Ducharme saw him rock the world in Lowell
when Rocky won the Golden Gloves, but Ducharme's
only strength was his strength. He was too slow
to duck a punch, too tough to not accept the harm
that punch after punch would do. A warrior-clown
who walked behind a trash truck for the city,
a beer-bellied Canuck who would not stay down.
Even flat on his back he scorned all pity.
Is he walking the streets today, or has he died?
Ducharme who sensed we live in myth not time.

Visions of Gerard at the Kerouac Monument

I'm following Gerard and Ti Jean down
Aiken Street toward the bridge. Gerard
has the tail of his mouse in a cardboard
box. His sick little mouse the cat pounced on.
"Little Kerouac mouse why didn't you run?"
They're shivering but they must find God.
Ti Jean has questions. Is God a fist or a rod?
Saintly Gerard knows. His will will be done.

I follow them across the bridge into town.
Gerard takes his brother's hand. "Ti Jean,
God's a printer like Pa, and we're his words,"
and then a lamb-white angel comes down
and sad Ti Jean wanders on alone to see
his words in stone, Gerard watching from the curb.

Lowell's Irish Micky Ward

Round 2. Ward's left eye is already cut
but he keeps moving toward Arturo Gatti.
My wife's gone to bed and turned out the light.
Gatti's left hook sounds like a thunderclap.
I haven't watched a fight in many years,
not since I moved far away from Lowell.
A Celtic Cross glistens on Ward's shoulder.
I wince as he shakes off blow after blow.
He has my uncle Leo's fighter's face,
with features almost as flat as a stone.
Staggered by a right he picks up the pace.
I want to see a hurt Gatti go down.
They fight to a draw. Closed eye for closed eye.
I go to bed shamefaced and stubbornly tribal.

Hoare's Fish Market

I walked to the market with my father
most Fridays to buy four pieces of cod
wrapped in paper soaked with grease
by the time we got back to our kitchen
where my mother and sister were waiting.
If times were good, my father bought
a piece for a neighbor who always called
it hake or skate if he just wanted to argue.

Mr. Hoare, our Neptune in tall boots,
watched over it all: haddock and cod,
halibut and tuna, swordfish and salmon
all laid out on an endless bed of ice.
When he spoke, you heard the distant sea
with its vast multitudes that would always be.

Sunday Morning

Come down and do your crossword. I worry
when you stay in bed. Last night's early frost
killed the sweet peas but not our patch of berries.
Seven across might just be Limberlost.
The morning paper says a man with Alzheimer's
has wandered off to find his long dead wife.
He told an aide he knows just where to find her.
All he took with him is a butter knife.
Hurry down. I want to see you grimace
when you might be stumped. Five down is breath.
The morning is quickly turning cold and grim.
Do you remember a Mary Elizabeth?
The raspberries in your berry bowl
are bright red and firm and very, very cold.

Forsythia

In Memory of Carleton Campbell

Ever since your surprised heart gave out
far too soon on that dark January afternoon,
I've been trying to get you down on paper:
Your deep love of all that was well made
how you could hold a rusty piece of metal
to the light and touch the hand that forged it.
You, a nurse beyond the uniform you wore,
knew the moon could pull us from our orbit
or cause the glacial earth to shudder underfoot.

A little homesick and a continent removed,
our dropped r's still clinging to us like burrs,
we shared only the Concord River when we met.
You knew its meadows, and I its final fall.
Carl, the forsythia you grew from a cutting
to replace our stunted one will bloom this year.
Standing by it, I see you drifting on our river,
water dripping slowly from your resting oars
as the current takes you to a golden shore.

Pollywog Pond

We learned how to skate there.
Boys on black. Girls on white.
Drawn to each other like those
small Scotty dogs on magnets
you could buy at the five and ten.
At first we could barely stand
and fell if no one held our hand,
but we soon learned to skate
in circles with hands held behind
our backs the way the adults did,
or we held on at the end of a whip
knowing someone would catch us
before we tumbled to the ice.
When we sat unlacing our skates,
the moon was a clock with no hands.

At the End

A cloudless dawn. My father's about to cross
the Pawtucket Bridge below the falls.
His black hair is slicked back. His gait is firm.
My mother's riding on the back of a motorcycle
holding tight to the boy who will become my sister's
father before he disappears like mist, but for now
the whole world is her oyster, and there's my sister
standing on one long leg before a full-length mirror
and Aunt Irene climbing the hill to Mrs. Costello's
kitchen where she's a trusted companion and servant
and I'm about to wake to the sound of heavy wagon
wheels turning on cobblestones and Mr. Goldman
the ragman singing "a-rags, a-rags, help an old man."
And no one yells "Christ-killer" from the curb.

3.

from

BRIDGE STREET AT DUSK

Pool Shark

He was an ancient gambler long absent
from the window table where the game
became a way of life, a badge of honor
where only the best were invited to play.
Dim-eyed and reptilian, Willie Provencher
sat on his favorite bench near the door
scanning the room for fish, and we came
duck-tailed and dumb from school to lose
at eight-ball to that dank and wrinkled shark
who held a dime store magnifying glass
to his best eye to line his shot before he slowly
chalked his cue then smiling ran the table.
He took our palm-wet quarters one by one.

A fingerling anxious for the sea, I left that world.
There's no small change in this Alaskan city
where I live. Crude oil sets my table now
and sharks wear silk not threadbare overcoats,
a place where few will bend to pick a quarter up.
I can see the earth's inviting bend toward Asia
and from time to time when moonlight falls
through clouds as thin as window glass,
I long to shine like bait in Willie's hand.

Manny

He was a minor god of the underworld
whose euphonious name brought no reply
if mentioned during the day, a lounge
singer, a maestro of sirens and bleary-eyed
last calls, of broken hearts and hands.
Still wearing his brushed velvet jacket
and heavy rouge, he joined us at a diner
that never closed, where laughter rang hollow
and everyone who came in eyed the clock.
His hair was dyed the color of Apollo's
and his voice was raw from singing requests.
He would sit on a stool at the long counter
or in a booth with men who might turn on him
once the night melted like lard on a griddle.

Women Waiting, 1942

Slant light, the light Vermeer taught us
how to see, falls upon three women
standing outside Lowell's railroad station
where it appears a train has just arrived.
They wear dark winter coats that narrow
at the waist the way an hourglass narrows.
The tallest one seems no stranger to sorrow.
Her face alone is turned to face the camera.
Another holds a white box tied with string,
a treat perhaps. The third wears an apricot-
colored hat tilted so to almost touch one ear.
New snow is on the station's iron roof.
Light and shadow, the secrets of the heart.
They stand together and they stand apart.

Men Waiting, 1942

Three men wearing heavy woolen coats
stand in shadow away from the slant light
that falls on the women in their photograph.
The oldest, the one holding a stubby pipe,
is wearing a working man's cloth cap
the kind only a poseur would wear today.
Their faces are as worn as the cobblestones
in the street. After a decade of hard times
war is now dealing the cards. On a peeling
poster on the station's wall behind the men
a hula dancer is swaying to the tune of Ray
Kinney's "Aloha Maids." The men look
out of the frame toward something unseen.
A single bulb lights the station's waiting room.

Victory in Europe (8 May 1945)

When the voice on the radio proclaimed V-E
Day, my mother turned it off and got down
the large bowl she used to make oleomargarine
and the wooden spoon we used to mix yellow
coloring into the lard-colored brick. The spoon
was a hoe in my small hand when I helped
so I watched. Her knuckles turned white
as she mixed. I listened for my uncle Tosi
coming up the stairs with his duffle bag over
his shoulder before I remembered he wasn't
coming back from some place called Anzio
for Wonder Bread spread with oleo and jam.
"Who wants butter when you can have oleo?"
he'd say to my mother and offer me a slice.
I watched her mix until the moon appeared
in a sky that was both clear and bitterly cold.

Gypsies, Lower Belvidere, 1947

A handwritten sign reading *Fortunes Told*
appeared on a grim November afternoon
in a store window uphill from Gormley's
diner. Instead of going home after school
we walked back and forth watching a girl,
a child, I realize now, sitting at a table
in the window and slowly shuffling a deck
of cards. Her long dress was apple-red.

An older woman watched us from the door.
Neighbors paused but no one went inside.
Within a week, the window was dark again.
We never found the trap door leading to the river
where a stolen car full of other gypsies waited,
only a stained army blanket, a child's rag doll.

Pollywogs

The old photograph where Joey Duffy has his arm
over my shoulder as if we were buddies just home
from a great adventure has turned a yellowish-brown.
It must have been a birthday party. The low stone
wall behind us is a neighbor's. Was this before
we set out without a word to anyone for Pollywog
Pond only to be brought back to our mothers
in a police car with its siren going? We were gods
in the neighborhood for a day. Duffy and Sexton
explorers. When did he begin to build the wall
he disappeared behind, stone by invisible stone
until no one could follow him, no one at all?
At night, we watched for shooting stars with tails
like pollywogs swimming in the bottom of a pail.

Sister Rose of Lima

The school's oldest nun when we were her class
when she already had one foot firmly in heaven
where angels converse in Irish accented Latin.
We bragged we didn't care if we failed or passed.
Our only goal was to avoid being the last
one down the stairs, or the first one to spin
the classroom's globe from its axis, snatch a pin
from a classmate's hair or pretend to fast.
One morning we cut the head off a doll
filled it with ketchup and rolled it toward
her desk. We heard her weeping in the hall
after she turned and fled the room. Now more
than fifty years later departing my own fall
for winter, I think once more of *Infernus* of Hell.

Silver Mittens, Immaculate Conception, CYO

Friday nights, the old CYO Hall on a bluff
where two rivers come together glowed
like a ship about to set sail leaving behind
a world worn down by constant want and worry.
A boxing ring was set up on the basketball court,
the Holy Grail to boys dreaming of dancing
across its canvas like their hero Willie Pep.

Narrow shouldered with hands as small as a girl's
I practiced hooks and jabs in my bedroom
until I was chosen to climb into that ring
and point to the winning boxer's corner.
From there I looked down upon row after row
of men and boys all wearing crew cuts as flat
as a field of wheat, girlfriends coiled like springs.

Pin Boy at the Rex

When only a few people were bowling
he perched on the shelf behind his lane
like an owl. When bored, he began to sing
or sip from the flask he'd hidden away.

People said he longed to be a jockey
when he was a boy, but that was long ago,
like so many dreams it was now in hock
and the ticket long lost, a broken bow.

There were nights when someone tried
to clip him when his back was turned
to impress a girlfriend or just for spite —
to give him a close shave, a little razor burn,

but he always stepped aside like Fred Astaire,
if Astaire had one good eye and snow-white hair.

Remembering Lowell's Lines on a Winter Morning

Opening the door before dawn to deep snow
that began overnight, the first true snow of winter,
I'm a child again unschooled in grief or loss,
innocent of letters carved in cold stone
a boy trying his best to memorize one stanza
of a poem. *The snow had begun in the gloaming*
and busily through the night, lines I would stutter
then forget when my time came to recite
in class. *Had been heaping field and highway.*
I can see headlights moving on the road.
When the kettle comes to a boil it's time
to have my breakfast. Beyond the window
where the clouds have begun to thin, blur of stars
and then the moon. *With a silence deep and white.*

Bessie's Store

The door to the room where they lived opened
and Bessie, club-footed and small as a child,
came out to see what I wanted. She sighed.
I was after kerosene for our parlor stove
and she knew I had no money, only a note.
I heard her husband coughing from behind
the door. He was as thin as a worn dime
and never said a word. Bessie never said no.
In her brown sweater, she could have been a crab
the way she moved one way and then the other
across the floor for a can of Spam or to grab
Wonder Bread from a wobbly shelf near the door
that had one dusty window that dimmed the stars
that were to a child, fireflies in a heavenly jar.

Tulips

Tulips now opening in a neighbor's yard
and I'm a boy once again on the dark back
stairs from our apartment on my way to fill
my wagon with tulips from the garden
of a doctor's stone house. I tossed and turned
all night dreaming of the yellow ones with
a red flame on every petal, a bright flame
that reminded me of the votive candle
I'd soon be lighting. Was it beauty or greed
that drove me the way it drove those Dutch
traders mad with desire for the rarest bulb?
It was raining lightly and the street
was slick as I eased my wagon down the hill
taking great care that my treasure didn't spill.

That Other Door

I'm there again behind the wheel of our Ford
the one with the handbrake that doesn't hold,
the one with bald tires turned to the curb
as I race through curve after dangerous curve
the way they do in the movies. No goggles.
No leather helmet on my head, only my loyal dog
beside me on the seat for company, then I
spy my father coming up the hill with a lilac
branch in his hand. Almost home, he falls
and pointing toward the rising moon calls
Harriett and my mother appears. *You're drunk,*
is all she says. *You're drunker than a skunk.*
Branch in hand she helps him across the kitchen floor,
but he's already gone through that other door
the one that will lead him in time to another room
to die alone, without a home, without that moon.

A Second Snow

Snow fell all that windless night
like the flour sifted for the cake
my mother was certain to make
if school was canceled to my delight.

Some sixty years later I watch it snow
all night because I cannot sleep.
I watch it cover the road like a sheet.
I watch as the wind begins to blow.

The Final Chapter, 1958

If you pleased Miss Shanley in class with your
desire to be businesslike and your knowledge
of merchandizing, how a window should look
from the street, when to smile and never frown
the way she did looking down with Olympian
disgust at my D.A., pegged pants, and Mr. B collar,
greasy from hair that looked like it had been
washed in axle grease, then you might be
sent for an interview near the end of senior
year to be a stock boy or the boy who helped
change the front windows after closing time.
I had change and a church key in my pocket
and didn't need to kneel before a mannequin.
On the morning she declared, "This is the final
Chapter," she appeared to look at me and smile.
Miss Shanley, a well-placed mirror holds no shadow.

October's Ghost

What was the name of my classmate who fell
through thin ice one night in late October
of the year we were learning how to spell?
Our first loss, missing footprints in the snow
at recess. Now when the leaves begin to fall
I think of her again caught under that ice,
her small mouth filling as she tries to call
out, not understanding what it means to die.
Was she the girl all in white who placed
the crown of violets on the Virgin Mary's
head in the schoolyard on the first of May,
the girl who tripped and scraped one knee?
The moon overhead seems as thin as ice
tonight. Dear ghost comfort me when I die.

The Gleaners

Heavy morning mist rising from the river
beyond the railroad tracks where boxcars
once waited on a spur behind the Bridge
Table factory where ancient women, dressed
in black from head to toe, picked up scraps
of wood to burn, women who reminded me
of the print of Millet's painting, *The Gleaners*.
Even now when I see a woman all in black
I think of them. A block from the factory,
they knelt in church every morning saying
the rosary in Lithuanian. Their church is gone,
but I sense them moving toward me in the mist
like figures at the end of an old movie reel
who vanish in a flash of light, shadow the dark.

Wamesit Falls

Branches and debris
in the Concord

River where Oliver
Whipple made gun-

powder so fine
it was better

than gold coin
when filling a

ship's deep hold
with African slaves;

early one morning
in 1820,

the mill exploded
and poor Tom

Sullivan, father of
Mary and Rose

went up like
a Chinese rocket,

a few beads
from the rosary

he no longer
needed were all

that came back
down, not even

a singed ear.
If you come

this way on
a clear night,

look for him
in the curled

lip of water
in the stars.

St. Joseph's Boys School

"My own play '33 A Musical Sketch" on the back
of the photograph where five boys pose for posterity.
The one wearing a grownup's fedora is Jack Kerouac.
Martin, Drolet, Parent, and Lessard are lost
to us now like the blackface two of them wear.
Kerouac is fingering what appears to be a lyre.
Notice Drolet's starched collar and cauliflower ears.
Catholic schoolboys, they're God's chosen choir.
The school is long gone. Canadian French no longer
fills the streets or rises cheek to jowl from tenements
along the polluted Merrimack. I saw Kerouac long ago
on Back Central, dead drunk, his pocket money spent
on hangers-on or pissed away, swaying from side
to side in moonlight as if to the music of that lyre.

Rochette's Diner

Perhaps because it's a cold Saturday afternoon
I imagine it's the 50's, and I'm going to buy
beans from Rochette's Diner, small and pale
spooned onto a plate, beans my friend Big Al,
Alphonse to his family, covered with butter
then spread cold on white bread for breakfast
after a long night of going from bar to bar,
beans his ancestors lived on when they came
down from Quebec for work in the now idle
mills, beans he said were beginning to grow
where he planted them in a plot by the coop
where his father kept his Rhode Island Reds.
He'd climb hand over hand right out of Lowell
one of these days. Did I want to come along?

Tannery Bridge

If snow that fell during the winter was still
on the ground in April, the river began to rise.
When it rained hard, we couldn't get our fill
of watching it come up both day and night.
We stood on the bridge below the tannery
that crossed to factories on the other side.
It shuddered and groaned when rammed
by a log or a barrel much to our delight,
and if it continued to rise, the local cops
would tell us to go home. We stood our ground
waiting for one last chance to dash across
before the water peaked and began to go down.
Soon we were crossing without glancing down
to where our ordinariness for a moment drowned.

The Church of the Immaculate Conception

Because the massive side door is slightly
ajar at 6 a.m., I decide to pay a visit,
to inhabit my past. Inside it could be night.
Old women kneeling. Perfume thick as mist.
To my surprise, the man with the purple-red
stain on half his face, a birthmark or a wound
from his war, is still sitting alone at the end
of a pew, a man who disappeared as soon
as Mass was over, barely pausing to bend
one knee, his close-cropped hair now snow.
Penance is the only coin that's never spent.
He could be a shadow or even a ghost.
I genuflect. Touch the pew. Turn around to go.
Unclench my fist. Drop a few coins in the box.

These Lines

He would have been at home with the Irish
who dug the canals so Lowell could prosper,
men who knew life ends with keening not sighs.
One brother lost to the river, another to war,
and both parents long dead. His wife would die
too young leaving him five children to raise
in cold-water flats while sirens howled at night
and hunger sat at their table day after day.
He was no longer the youth hitting the bag
at the CYO Hall from dawn to dusk until it split,
who jumped rope until the floor began to sag.
Life knocked him down. He refused to quit.
He's with his dead now. The canals flow shallow.
These lines I write for my uncle, Leo Quinn.

Amerikay, 1832, a Letter

When your ship sails into Boston Harbor
stay with those who are walking to Lowell
by road or along the bank of the canal
that goes from Charlestown to the Paddy Camps.
I helped dig it when I came over. They need servants.
Don't speak Irish. Drown it like an unwanted kitten.
Answer when they call you Bridget. They can't
imagine we have our own names or our own spit.
No Lord owns the sky or the clouds overhead.
Don't let them laugh at you like that poor Bridget
who begged the druggist for the glory of rhyme
when sent by her mistress for chloride and lime.
Sister, bend like a rowan on a windswept ridge.
Be as bright as the halo around the Virgin's head.

Boiler Rooms, Boott Mills

The man in front of the massive boiler
wears the dull green shirt and trousers
worn by laborers, a green that mocks
the very idea of spring. Above his head
a vast continent of gauges and asbestos
covered pipes that leave a fine gray dust
on his shoulders. If his final destination's
that other hell, he'll need to bring a sweater
but there's no hint of self-pity in his gaze.
I imagine that his look is that of Charon
picking up his long pole on his way to work
rowing the wailing dead across the River
Acheron for the coin beneath each tongue,
both of them doing what needs to be done.

Charon

Night after night, Charon hoped that he could
catch a little shuteye after the graveyard shift
was over before the dead, soiling themselves
and trying to slip out of line and disappear,
came down the slope to the river once again.
He was a company man and didn't complain.
But what was he to do with the coin placed
beneath each tongue. Visit Mount Olympus?
Hermes had given him the ears of a wolf
to wear so he could hear the dead coming.
He put them beneath his head for a pillow
and thought what a good friend Hermes is,
but as soon as he began to dream of figs dipped
in honey, the dead began howling on the shore.

The Wool Sorter

Day after day he sorted wool at the mill
into different grades. He had a good eye.
They said he was blessed with strong lungs
for a Greek. His black hair would turn lamb-
white before he began to cough. After work
he climbed three flights of stairs to where
his smiling children waited to hear another
tale of Jason's quest for the Golden Fleece.
They imagined it was his destiny to find it
hidden in a bale of wool that he was sorting.
They watched every morning from the window
as he crossed the bridge over the canal
that would take him to the river and the mill.
He was Jason setting sail with the dawn.

Praise Poem

Praise to Gummy Cullen who had no teeth
who held a cigarette inside his mouth
while he looked for a prime cut of beef
"on sale today" for women always down
on their luck. Praise to Oscar Denault
who could hang a side of beef on a hook
without help and cut a fly speck of fat off
for grumblers who seldom came back.
Praise to Mary French wrapping on the line
the day the saw cut Gummy's fingertip
off. Mary who scooped it up with a sigh
stuck it back on and wrapped it with a bit
of slip, and praise to the prized green meat
we took home, praise to sawdust beneath our feet.

Walden Pond

The sky was clear and pine needles
covered the path to where Thoreau
built his cabin on the morning I saw
mist rising from a cove like a ghost
and found myself thinking of that Irish
Bog trotter, James Collins, who sold
his shanty by the railroad tracks
to Thoreau for twenty-four dollars,
Collins who was last seen walking west
just as dawn was breaking with everything
he owned tied in a bundle on his back.
Walking behind were his wife and children
and the scrawny chickens that had spied
a man circling the shanty like a fox.
May he always have a roof for the rain.
May the sun shine bright on his windowpane.

Homage to Lorine Niedecker

After a night scrubbing floors at the hospital,
after the ride home with one eye on the gauge,
she'll open the warped door to her house.
Her coat still on, she'll start a fire in the stove.
When the heavy iron kettle sings, she'll make
a cup of tea with a little milk and one sugar.
"Three cups from a bag," her dead mother will say.
"The golden goose don't live on Blackhawk Island,
Lorine, just remember that." When the bag stops
dripping she'll put it in a spoon and carry her
chipped cup to a table by the kitchen window.
Outside, above her father's shed, she'll see
the pale moon, a laborer's moon, that's her lamp.
Warm now, she'll begin to stitch then unstitch a poem
as if it were a dress. Her eyelids droop then close.

The American Dream

From a block-long empty lot where mills
still stood when I was young, I watch light
fall on the far bank of the Concord River,
light that must have fallen through high
windows on workers stealing a moment
to read a worn letter from home, perhaps
in Irish saying *I'm glad Liam found you work*
in the dye house, your father's had a little fall,
or a later one in Greek saying *Bless you*
daughter, the landlord's paid, we breathe.
Intertwined voices on the stairs at dawn
climbing to learn the language of bobbin and loom.
Wind lifts a few scraps of paper from the lot.
They rise, swirl about, catch the light, fall back.

For Sean Sexton of Coolmeen

While visiting Limerick, I read in the paper
how you discovered nine of your cows
dead in the high pasture when you went
to gather them for the evening's milking,
how you led the singed and blind survivor
down to the barn where it bawled all night.
Why lightning from a quickly clearing sky?
Why the heifer bought with all your savings?

If I had driven out to Coolmeen, we could
have watched the western sky for comets,
celestial debris our poor ancestors called
the tears of saints. And naked, painted
like ancient Gaels, we could have walked
the hills reciting the misfortunes of our name —
the cattle stolen and the ancient tower sacked
until the heaving sea itself was wet with tears.

Tableau

The young woman's eyes are on the infant
in the stroller a man is pulling up
the steep steps leading to St. Patrick's
while she lifted and pushed from below
before they paused to catch their breath.
Notice if you will the cold November rain.
Because she's standing on tiptoe you can
see the worn heels of her shiny gold boots.
The hood of the man's sweatshirt's drawn tight
making him appear medieval, a little menacing.
He has something tattooed on his knuckles.
A few stragglers hurry by them. Mass has begun.

The Clock at City Hall

On its granite column it seems to almost
touch the stars from a certain angle,
tall enough that workers would know
when the day was done in mills that once
wove cloth from cotton picked by slaves;
the obelisk dedicated to Ladd and Whitney,
mill workers killed by a mob in Baltimore
on their way to Washington to answer
Lincoln's call to put down the rebellion,
is only steps away from where I stand
watching three young girls with ribbons
in their afros laughing as they run back
and forth collecting tossed scratch tickets
that their mother checks then throws away.

I can see the diner where I had breakfast.
When the cook asked the man beside me
how he was, he replied, "That fucking nigger got
elected again." Then he slammed his cup down.
A ring of large heavy keys hung from his belt.
A block away, a man walking a dog appears.
He pauses, looks at us and then at the clock
for a moment before he hurries down a side street
toward a loft with tall windows in what was once a mill.

In a Pine Grove by the River

Turning off the highway in a rented car
I soon come to the place where my father
came to wash and wax our old Cadillac,
wondering once again why I come back.
The Cadillac was as black as Pollard's
hearse and as tall as my father was tall.
When we were finished, we sat side by side
on a rusting running board in silence
while he drank a beer cooled by the river.
One quick sip always made me shiver.
If, as Longley wrote, *Home is a hollow
between the waves*, this was his only home.
For all our longing, for all our art
what do we ever know of the human heart?

The Whistler House Museum

I step out of the house where James
McNeill Whistler was born into slanting
rain, the kind that falls in his etchings.
"I will be born where and when I want,
and I do not choose to be born in Lowell,"
he said. My father's ghost is by my side.
"I was never in there when I was alive,"
he says. "I would have enjoyed it there
after work." He wants to know if I've
ever seen stars reflected in the canals
late at night. He has the tongue he never
had. Everything comes easy to us now.
We watch a slight Asian woman crossing
one of the bridges over the canals
engineered by Whistler's father to carry water
to the now decrepit mills where he worked
when first married. We stop for a bowl of pho.
"Imagine a mackerel snapper eating noodles,"
he says and laughs. Later, climbing the road
to the top of Fort Hill, we flush a cock pheasant.
He asks if I'll come back again. I say I will.

St. Patrick's Church

A young boy, Vietnamese I'm pretty sure,
has tucked a snowball up his sleeve.
He's a magician, and the snow's his dove.
A second ball and he's a juggler trying to lure
a shy girl a little closer. They seem so pure
and innocent like children in a snow globe.
The girl isn't falling for his act, and his gloves
are soon wet, so he vanishes through the door
of the church, an altar boy almost late for Mass
perhaps. I watch her drop a handful of snow
into the dark water of a canal dug by Irish
immigrants almost two centuries ago,
then she kneels and gathers more snow
that becomes a lotus blossom in her hands.

Bridge Street at Dusk

Almost dark. River mist covers the street,
the dull stuff of mill town after mill town.
Most of the storefronts are empty now.
Even the pawnbroker has locked his door.
In one, a woman is having her fingernails
lacquered while her friends wait their turn.
They wear the pale colors of hotel workers:
washed-out blues, grays, and dull yellows.
I watch her spread her hands like a peacock
spreads its tail to show its feathers to the world.
A young boy is nodding his head to the beat
of salsa music flowing from three speakers.
Laughter flows like water from a bucket.
Saturday night and the world belongs to them.

4.

ON BECOMING A POET

On Becoming a Poet

FOR MOST PEOPLE the place where they were born or where they grew up fades like an old black-and-white photograph as time passes, for some it refuses to fade no matter how far they wander. It gains depth and clarity year after year. I have lived in Alaska for most of my adult life, but it has never shaped me the way my hometown, Lowell, Massachusetts, did and still does. I have published several books of nature poetry and have an almost completed manuscript sitting in my desk, so I obviously have great affection for Alaska where I live, but Lowell, my "dear dirty Dublin" with apologies to James Joyce, remains closest to my heart.

I know little about my ancestors on either side except that they came to America from Scotland and Ireland and ended up in Lowell sometime in the nineteenth century probably because they heard there was work to be had. My father never talked about family that I can remember. My mother did visit her sisters and brother, but their parents had died when they were very young. I often wonder if my deep love of place might in some small way be compensation for that loss of a connection to the past.

I have long believed that if my Lowell poems can capture the working class people who walked its streets when I was growing up, if I can get them down right, I will have done them justice and helped me understand my own past a little better at the same time. When I can, I walk Lowell's streets accompanied by ghosts who can be surprisingly good company.

I left Lowell for the first time at 1 a.m. on a rainy February night in 1959 when a half-filled brown Army van picked me up then drove slowly along Central Street passing by the old post office where I had registered for the draft when I turned eighteen. I imagined the old buildings were sad to see me go. The only people on the street were a few wandering drunks.

The van delivered us a few hours later into the waiting arms of an unsmiling sergeant who was waiting for us at Fort Dix, New Jersey. After an expletive filled welcome, we were marched off to have our heads shorn and to discover that we were now a flock of sheep.

Being one of a flock of nameless sheep was better than my prospects in Lowell. After school was out for the day, I hung around the poolroom acting too cool to care about the future. I knew the location of a package store that would sell alcohol to a minor, and I had identification that claimed I was twenty-one when I was only sixteen. This gave me a kind of status. When I realized that the job running an elevator I managed to get at the local paper after I graduated from high school because my uncle Leo worked there as a printer was a dead end, I figured it was time to join the Army.

My parents did not see me off the night I left. My mother's late shift at the fish stick factory wore her out, and my father was not home yet. They might not have known exactly when I was leaving. My sister has told me she did not know I had enlisted until I was gone. Little did I know then that night was the first small step on my journey to Alaska and to becoming a poet.

It took a while to adjust to Fort Dix, but before long it seemed normal to wake to the sound of our barrack's door opening followed by a voice bellowing "Drop your cocks and grab your socks." I slept with my socks on so I was ahead of the game. I still remember one lanky redhead from Delaware who carried only two pictures in his wallet. One was of his parents and the other one was of his mule. He seemed to miss the mule more than he missed his parents. His name was Leathers, and he could never find his socks.

It was Leathers who spent hours trying to teach me the proper way to break down and then reassemble an M-1 rifle in a blink of the eye. I was all thumbs. I wish I had known Henry Reed's magnificent poem, "Naming of Parts" back then. That M-1 was my best friend according to our drill sergeant. Soon I was running through the woods at night with the other recruits cradling my best friend in my arms while yelling R.A. ALL THE WAY over and over even though many of my fellow recruits had been drafted and considered the rest of us a pack of fools for joining. Looking back, the army did have a way with rhyme.

As odd as this may sound, two of my barracks mates who had been drafted seemed to be always reading books when we were not running around in the woods or crawling under barbed wire. At least I found it odd.

One was a lawyer who had a degree in Literature from Syracuse. One night, the lawyer asked me, because my bunk was between their bunks, who I thought was the better writer, Henry Miller or Hemingway, no first name. I had no opinion about Henry Miller or Hemingway or any other writer, but I promised myself I would get one. I did not want to tell them that I was too shy to ask questions in school and my teachers must have assumed I was too dumb to learn much. Why would they have thought otherwise? I sat in the back room looking out the window or dropping my pencil on the floor. Today I would answer: I prefer Fitzgerald to either and then ask what they thought of Kerouac's early writing.

All things come to an end even basic training. Eight weeks later with a name tag on my fatigues to separate me from the nameless, I graduated from basic training and moved on to clerical school. I had taken a typing class in my senior year. I was the only male in the class. I still suspect the army sent those who would not survive advanced infantry or any kind of technical training to clerical school. When I fired a mortar round a second too early on the firing line at dawn one morning, my fate was sealed. I was a clerk.

After a brief visit home when my eight weeks of clerical training ended, the last time I saw my mother alive, I was on my way to Fort Richardson, Alaska, outside of Anchorage. There I spent much of my free time at the base library reading everything I could get my hands on. The thought entered my head one day that I might want to be some kind of a writer, after all I was a company clerk, but keeping track of a couple of hundred mechanics and truck drivers who had no use for clerks unless they needed a favor put that idea on hold. They often needed a favor.

Another mentor was Private Thomas Curtis, an African American graduate of Harvard College, who became my roommate because as the company clerk I had a room to myself. For a few months I shared my room with Curtis. He had joined up to attend the Army's Language School. Along the way something went wrong and he ended up in the 521st Transportation Company. Curtis would listen to opera night after night on a small portable phonograph while writing in a journal then glancing at me with a look on his face that seemed to suggest I was hopeless, but that didn't stop him from telling me what I should be reading instead of drinking beer at the beer hall every night.

Tired of waiting for his case to be resolved, he took the matter into his own hands by sending his dress uniform to a cleaner in New York City. When he was asked during a surprise inspection where his uniform was, he replied New York, and handed a laundry ticket to a fuming 2nd Lieutenant. He was court martialed and soon discharged. I was a character witness in his defense, a shaking character witness. The surprising thing is I expected to be at least criticized for defending Curtis but not a word was ever said. I sometimes wonder if his court martial was a ruse, and Curtis was on his way to the Aleutians to spy on the Russians. It was the age of "better dead than red."

I never had another roommate. Looking back now, I realize Curtis' court-martial was a turning point for me, a transformation. It was the first time I had ever stood up and spoken against something I thought was unjust.

Those three men, Scala, Levine, and Curtis, showed me that there was more to life than managing to survive. It was not long after I returned to Lowell when my time in the service ended that I made my first feeble attempt at writing a poem. I did not know then that Robert Service was a poet not to be admired, so it was probably a bad imitation of one of his poems. We had a northern landscape in common.

Things were no better in Lowell. They might even have been worse, but I had changed. I let my hair grow and grew a beard to go with my military moustache. I joined the Socialist Party of America, admired Henning Blomen, smoked a pipe and carried a paperback of Camus' *The Stranger* wherever I went, but nothing else changed. For two years, I worked a series of dead-end jobs before I became a student at Northern Essex Community College in Haverhill where I was encouraged to write poetry by a wonderful teacher, Marlene Molinoff. Her encouragement led to my being the first editor of *Parnassus*, a student literary magazine that is still being published.

After Northern Essex came an English degree from Salem State thanks to the new Vietnam G.I. Bill followed by an MFA degree from the University of Alaska and a teaching career at the University's Anchorage branch where I established the Creative Writing program and was the first poetry editor for the *Alaska Quarterly Review*. I wrote little during my academic career. Teaching came first. It was like running an elevator, you showed up and did your job. My job lasted for twenty-four years.

The night before I left Massachusetts to return to Alaska in 1968, I married a wonderful woman who is content to live with a husband who takes long walks with her and the dog and spends the rest of the day writing and reading. A husband who considers three a crowd. It is not a glamourous life, but it is a deeply satisfying one.

The poem I consider my first real poem is about Lowell's New State Poolroom in the 1950's and the men who day after day climbed the narrow steps to its door from the shoe shops or from one of the few remaining mills to play pool with lawyers and shop owners. The poem begins in the poolroom and ends with an image of the Alaska Range bending toward Asia. Both of my worlds combined. My first version of that poem probably was written in 1970. The latest version is in this collection.

I spent a week in Lowell last year. I stayed at an Airbnb a block from Oak Street where I spent the most enjoyable years of my youth. I had a good visit, but the Lowell of my youth is gone. I wandered down to Danas' Luncheonette where the counter man, Peter Danas, had a poem he wrote about the destruction of St. Peter's Church a few blocks up Gorham Street taped to the wall behind the counter. The luncheonette's brick façade was falling and the roof was caving in. Standing there looking at the permanently locked door, I knew I would never complete another book of poems about my Lowell, and I did not feel sad.

On my way back to the bed and breakfast, I stopped at a restaurant beside a bridge over the Concord River where I had Mofongo and an amazing bottle of Dominican beer called Presidente and listened to music for a while. When I left I realized that the restaurant was near the bridge where I saw a doe leap from thin ice to safety on the far bank one afternoon when I was a boy.

In the morning as I was leaving, I noticed two children standing in front of the house across the street. They were waiting for a van to take them to school. I had heard and seen the yellow van the previous morning. An eyebrow of stained glass above the window where a woman was watching caught the early morning light.

A NOTE ON THE AUTHOR

Tom Sexton was born in Lowell, Massachusetts, and lived in the city through his high school years. He earned degrees at Northern Essex Community College and now-Salem State University, and then pursued graduate studies at the University of Alaska, where he stayed and founded the creative writing program at the Anchorage campus. He taught there for decades and co-founded the highly respected *Alaska Quarterly Review*. The author of many volumes of poetry, his most recent collections are *Li Bai Rides a Dolphin Home (2018)*, *A Ladder of Cranes (2015)*, and *For the Sake of the Light: New and Selected Poems (2009)*, all from the University of Alaska Press. His Lowell books are *A Clock with No Hands* and *Bridge Street at Dusk*. Among his honors are being appointed Poet Laureate of Alaska (1995-2000) and being named a Distinguished Alumnus of Lowell High School. Tom and his wife Sharyn have lived in Alaska since 1970. Recently, they have lived part-time on the coast of Maine.

Merrimack Valley Magazine wrote: "Each poem unveils something new, and at times breathtaking, about one of the Merrimack Valley's most diverse and interesting places... Sexton's characters, relationships, and places spring from the page, brought to life by a tiny gesture or minute detail."

The Georgia Review praised Tom Sexton's language as "clear without tricks of fancy moves, yet his directness is powerful, and the effects are human."